Rise Like A Phoénix

Carmen Barnett

BookLeaf Publishing

Presentation by *BookLeaf Publishing*

Web: www.bookleafpub.com

E-mail: info@bookleafpub.com

ISBN: 978-93-5721-319-6

First edition 2023

The Purpose Of The Cross

The purpose of the cross,
Is to save the loss;
It's God in the flesh, fresh from heaven,
Stepped down to earth.
Then the spirit was birthed,
Through Mary, a saviour in a stable;
It's the truth, not a fable.

The purpose of the cross may sound odd,
But it's so that our sins can be forgiven,, and reunite us back to God.
Jesus took the blame and the shame,
He was whipped within inches of his life;
It was worse than being slashed with a stanley knife.

Fornication, deprivation, lies, phedophile
The cries of a baby in a womb,
That was sent to an early tomb.
Jesus took our shame,
Yes he would of felt pain--
A nine inch nail driven through his vain,
But he didn't complain;
His love is insane.

The purpose of the cross some yell
No you go to hell.
We couldn't give a toss,
We're not lost.
I've got my honey by my side,
My big bad ride,
Just step aside and let me live my life.

The purpose of the cross ain't no joke,
It's for the black, white, the rich, the poor,
lesbian transgender, all kind of folk.
Now I've given you a clue,
You know what to do.
Give your life to Christ,
Don't ever think twice.
Just seek God's face,
Sip from the cup of His grace,
And no the power of the cross.

Standard

When you think about the magnitude of God,
It can sound a little odd;
And the things we've heard,
Absurd,
But it's by inspiration.
I make these declarations
When you have problems;
Only God can solve them.

He made the world in seven days,
Yes, raise your eyebrows and look amazed;
Just Standard.

He broke down the walls of Jericho,
Opened the prison gates for Paul and Silas,
didn't you know?
Just Standard.

The women with a issue of blood he stopped that
in a flash,
Turned water into wine, what more trash into
cash;
Just Standard.

His only son, he gave,
And after three days, raised him from the grave;

Just Standard.

Now listen to me--
No matter the infirmity,
If he split the red sea,
It shows His mastery;
It's not wizardry.
He's incredible,
He's ocean deep,
He's the general,
There's no one higher
Than Jehovah jirah.
He can quench the flame and out the fire,
My prince of peace, my Adonai;
If I get too deep I just wanna cry.

This miracle worka,
He'll never hurt yah.
He'll graft you in,
No matter the sin.
Just give it to Him,
You can't stop the hope,
You can't stop the love,
Our God is so dope.

Jehovah Jirah,
He has the power,
No matter the hour.
The Hebrew defender,

He’s the real deal,
And not a pretender.

A World With No Division

Acts 2:21 says it shall come to pass,
Whoever calls upon the name of the Lord shall be saved, so you better act fast.
Put your hand up, be the first and not the last--
It's within your reach, it's within your grasp.
Don't look downcast,
It's good news, the best-forecast;
Your life will change, see the contrast
like raising a mast.
God is awesome, multifaceted, who can surpass the way he operates,
He's transparent like glass.
Yes it's true, on the other side there is greener grass.
Pavements paved with gold, I heard it's so vast,
So it means when we get to heaven, we'll surely have a blast.
More over there'll be no division there, there'll be no class,
You'll be happy and accepted, no longer an outcast.
When you meet Jesus, you can say bonjour, hola, or yes my boss--
Thank you for dying for my sins and trespass
What a feat, what a task;
I'm with my God at last.

God's More Than A Feeling

I use to pine after love,
Dine and drink wine after love,
Now I feel fine with a love;
Not rejected or dejected, what a love!

Like a stick of Blackpool rock,
No matter where you chop,
You can see the name;
Well I feel no shame.
Like Jeremiah, to say you're in my blood, you're in my vein;
I can't break this chain,
From old testament to new--
A God who is relentless and has pursued
The thing he made, me and you.

That's why on this gospel I will chew,
Passing it from me, on to you--
Saying what Jesus has done,
That powerful battle he's won,
To redeem you from sin,
And change you within.
There is no mistake,
You better rise and awake,
Don't debate,
It's your soul satan wants to take;

This news is real and not a fake,
He's not your friend, he's not your mate,
He wants to take you to that lake.

But there is a plan, there is a way,
Call out the name Jesus, and just say
"I believe you're the son of God";
It's supernatural it's not odd,
It's the powerful, wonderful word of God.
It all started and will end with God,
Yes, that ruler in the sky.
Just because you can't see him with your eye,
Don't be fooled, just give him a try.
He wants you to live, and never die.
It's not radical,
Or fanatical,
His love is ideal,
That's why I say it with passion and zeal;
God's more than a feeling he's real.

Where Will I Be

Where will I be,
When Jesus comes back for me?
Will I be in the rave smoking dope,
Sipping on Bacardi or drinking coke?
Will I be following my friends like a slave to the rhythm?
Or getting into all types of ism schism?
I know it ain't no joke,
But the young
Just wanna have fun.

My Nan
Who's a Christian
Often shouts, "Get your heart right,
Before Jesus comes back like a thief in the night!"
Then, I think about my fancy clothes and I yell,
"Don't preach at me,
I'm in my D&G,
Look at my figure in Hilfiger,
Louis Vuitton;
From top to bottom,
Gucci, Jimmy choo,
What do you want me to do?
Give it all up and follow you?
No can do.

Versace the best brand,
Don't you understand?
Sorry, right now, Prada is my heavenly father!"

Two weeks later,
I follow my nan to church to appease her.
The worship is sweet,
I even found my self tapping my feet
And loving the gospel beat,
The preacher's preaching how the world has gone mad,
And so many people rejecting God;
All of a sudden, I even felt odd.

I wondered if I declared and decree,
Would God save a sinner like me?
Then a soft voice said, "That's why I hung on a tree,
Change your life and come follow me.
I'll set you free,
Give you a new identity,
A better destiny;
Then you'll no longer have to worry where you'll be.

Decide Your Track

It's about King Jesus coming back,
So you need to decide your track.
When he ascended to the sky,
It was just a temporary goodbye.
Will it be like the day of Noah when God sent the rain?
It was insane.

Will you be sexting or texting or sipping champagne
Will you be on the phone to your hun, chewing gum
Or wiggling your bum
Or will it be oh just leave me man?
Can't you see I'm a babe with my tiny waist,
Pretty face,
And good hair?
Why should I care?

What about you,
What you gonna do?
Will you reject the Christ
That sacrificed
To give you life?

We're living in revelation
With trails and tribulation,
Do you have time to wait?
Take satan's bait,
Why risk a fate
Of being thrown in the lake.

Will you still be talking Brexit,
Or watching Netflix?
Let's face it,
You might look slick,
Know how to talk politics,
But when put to the test--
Your life's a mess,
You sleep around,
Don't be too proud, or you will be going down.

But for those of us who believed,
And were not deceived,
We wait with anticipation
Whilst building relation,
And overcoming all kinds of situations.

Tell me what you gonna do
When Jesus judges you,
Will it be well done my child?
Or please don't cramp my style.

Time is promised to no one;
If you become a christian,
Your life's not done.
It's a different fun,
You're a friend of Christ,
Life's twice as nice.
Just bow your knee,
And say after me,
"I repent.";
And believe these words are heaven sent.

The Remedy

There's an infectious disease called sin,
A precarious condition Adam and Eve put us in.
We've tried this, and we've tried that;
We can't eradicate sin, it's multiplied like rats.

But there is a remedy, there is a cure;
Jesus, so righteous, and so pure.
There's no extracts,
Check out these facts--
He's the only one that can manage,
To repair the damage;
He has the healing, the anointing,
Don't that sound soothing?

There's no other God who's performed countless miracles,
Read the bible, it will send shivers down your spine like icicles.
He opened the eyes of the blind,
Turned water into wine.
Converted the thief on the cross,
Pure excitement not chaos.

He amassed such a following,
If he was on insta, it would be ka-ching.
His brain is more than wikipedia,

Any encyclopedia.
You can't count the information he can feed yah.
He'd break the internet,
Bill Gates or Einstein can't match his intellect;
His accolades are endless,
Don't take my word, put him to the test.
He is the doctor that can cure any disorder,
His miracles are endless, like running water.
Jesus is the protein, the substance,
He can cure us in an instance;
It's not science.

Now with this data,
You should run from sin, say bye, chow see you later.
You'll never regret it that's for sure,
If you take this Jesus, the remedy, the cure.

Yourself

When you dress yourself
And comb your tress yourself
Do you assess yourself?
And confess to yourself,
"I look a mess" to yourself?

Do you look at the excess to yourself
Flat chest big chest to yourself,
Then jest to yourself
"If only I could compress my self,
I'd be less depressed with myself,
And stop inflicting this stress to myself."

When you come too, do you address yourself?
When you've processed to yourself,
"Perhaps I'm too obsessed with myself",
I need to impress upon myself,
To stop this bitterness to myself.

It's time, I should think the best of my self,
I may not win the contest,
Certainly not the largest,
But I'm a beautiful empress.
I may not be able to bench press,
But I can rock a red dress.
I will speak words to bless,
Work hard and bring success to myself.

Your Life Matters

Begging, please Lord please,
When will my struggle cease?
Each day seems like hurdle after hurdle,
You cry, why is my life a vicious circle?
Each day I get up, I grumble;
"Will this rat race
That I face,
Keep gathering pace?
Or will it end when I end?"

How can my life matter,
When it's always in tatters.
Life, a broken down fence,
It makes no sense,
From generation to generation,
I'm filled with indignation.
A dot, an ugly spot,
Who gives a jot if I rot?

I feel like I can no longer fight,
Then I see a light,
You come to my aide
And whisper, "You are fearfully & wonderfully made,
Unique, and set apart,
I knitted you from the start;

Created you in my image,
You're a blessing not a baggage."

O Lord, I repent.
My despise is such an offence.
Why did I look and resent
When you created me with such reverence?
I was feeling down and battered,
I wanted to be altered;
But now I've heard your word,
I'm no longer perturbed,
No matter the status,
Or because of the peoples' bias,
No one's a disaster,
All lives truly matter.

It's So Emotional

I feel so dissed, so rejected,
So deeply and utterly affected.
The pain inside
Is like a roller coaster ride,
A slippery slide,
In whom can I confide.

I thought you were so passionate,
So truly affectionate;
I would never have done what you've done,
You were my boo, you were my hun,
But you picked me up and spat me out for fun.
So callous, so ice cold,
So many people you told--
Now on social media, I'm trolled.

I can't show my face in public,
This has really knocked me for six.
What you've done is so misogynistic,
The signs were there, you were so chauvinistic.
A pig, a sexist,
Always putting me in 'my place'.
Shoving me, and slapping my face,
I hid, and waited for my bruises to fade
Till there wasn't a trace,
The stress has made me a real basket case.

When will I be free
From this overwhelming anxiety?
It's just not me,
I'm normally strong and carefree,
So confident and happy,
But like a candle I'll burn bright again.
I won't make your cruelty my bane,
I'll erase it from my brain.
Bury it like a funeral,
But I can't lie, it's so emotional.

What Is Happiness

What is happiness?
Is it hope built on nothing less
Than looking your best,
Having bags of money to invest,
A stunning figure, strong arms or big chest?

Is happiness living in the best post code?
Having someone daily sweep your road?
Is it having power to command;
Click your fingers and make demands?
Or is it being with someone of your dreams,
2 point, 4 kids, and a dog, what a team!

Is it being able to laugh everyday;
Having no problems just trouble free and gay?
Is it getting your own way,
Clap your hands and people obey
Because you have a mansion, Bugatti and a rare
Chevrolet?

I've seen the rich in Beverly Hills,
Smoke pot, drink shots and down deadly pills;
There in Gucci, Versace but still unhappy.
Their house look so grand,
With acres of land,
But still they're not happy.

On facebook, instagram,
With millions of fans,
There forever searching, I still can't understand;
Is there anything that will ever please man?
Then I deduced like Solomon, the wisest one
Who worked out a plan,
Without God, happiness is futile, put him to the test.
He'll clean you up, and take away the mess.
This is the conclusion, this I confess;
It's only through God, you'll find true happiness.

Defying Societal Norms

Don't be afraid to be different and stand out,
You don't have to be quiet invisible or loud;
But just be good,
Like you know you should--
Standing up for what's right,
Even if it feels like you won't win the fight.

Everyone is unique,
Though some are made to feel like a freak--
Society wants you to conform,
To a norm,
Fashion trends,
To fit in with your friends,
Hair, nails, Mercedes Benz;
No matter where you turn it's on every end.

Stand up, don't stand down,
Be strong, stand your ground.
Maintain your self respect,
Even if it hurts and you feel like a social reject.
The pain you feel,
It's hard, it's real.
Your self esteem takes a hit,
It's deep in your stomach, it's sunken to the pit.

The good news is you're still alive;
Yes you've survived,
Like a phoenix you've arised.
Some look shocked, some so surprised,
Well done you, you've opened their eyes.
This is where the power lies,
Don't feel torn to conform,
It's not always cool to fit the norm.

Who Is Your Influencer

These days, the power of an influencer is
immense;
The money they make, extravagance and
expense,
Just don't make any sense.
But we all want someone to follow,
It's in us, sometimes, we're shallow.

Whatever the news, or the views,
You can pick, choose, and refuse.
An influencer is in demand,
The popularity and respect they command
Has raised their status,
Fans turn to them more than they do a thesaurus.

They pick their niche,
Work tirelessly to outreach;
Then become inspirational,
Some truly sensational.
Like the most famous I know--
Jesus, the star of the show;
Top notch celebrity,
The best in publicity.
With power to affect,
The highest elect,
There's no other influencer,
That can ever measure.

Your Worth

No matter who you are,
You can aim for the star.
Even if you were born in the mud,
You can flower and bloom like a bud.
You can't see the wood for the trees,
And all you want to do is cry and fall to your knees;
You should know, you're valuable here on earth.
Know your worth.

When You're Sinking

When you're sinking, are you thinking how did you get here?
As life immersed you, or cursed you because you didn't adhere?
You hold your hands high to the sky for someone to come to your rescue,
But no one sees you, it's getting desperate, what do you do?
Now you're fully submerged, the situation is getting worse, you're turning blue.
You don't want to perish, should you have cherished the life given you.

Then you awake;
Someone has resuscitate,
And changed your fate.
You're alive,
So glad you've survived,
Now able to breath,
Your soul's been retrieved.
It gets you thinking,
"Who's saved me from sinking?".

Break Free

Being in bondage without no rope,
Ain't no joke;
Restrained,
And in chains,
Tied to that thing,
Someone's put you in.

Who has taken hold of your mind?
What has you restricted, so tightly confined?
Your hands and feet are not bind,
Yet you struggle for the freedom you want to find.

There's no doubt something is gripping your mind,
You have eyes but you can't see, you're literally blind.
Who will release you from this horrible torment?
Make up your mind, don't lament,
Break the chain before it sets like cement.
Run to safety from confusion,
For darkness to Christ is the solution.

Panic Demic

When the first lockdown was announced I
thought, "Is someone taking the mick?",
And if they are, that's really sick.
Suddenly there was another killer for 2020 on
the loose,
First it was bombings, shootings then stabbings,
what the deuce.
This one's more deadly, and has bought the
world to its knees,
Day by day the death's toll has increased.

It's Corona aka Covid 19,
Deadlier than a cobra, rapid like bullets from a
magazine.
It's infectious, treacherous, and wastes whom it
pleases;
Government or scientists can't say when it will
cease.

The stock market and the economy has taken a
bash,
You can't get toilet roll, sanitizer or hand wash.
All types of food people will stash,
As soon as the shelves are restocked, they're
empty in a flash.
NHS staff overworked and feeling harassed,

They're rushed off their feet,
No gloves, no masks, whatever next, no food to eat.

This wasn't forecasted, no one predicted a global spread;
How much more can we take, we can't keep counting the dead.
What's the solution
To this untimely intrusion?
There is a scripture so profound,
I like how it sounds.
It's direct from God, hear what he says,
"If my people, called by my name, humble themselves and pray,
And turn from their wicked ways,
Then will I hear from heaven & forgive their sins and heal their land.".
My o my don't that sound grand!

It's not something trending,
It's a word from the king.
Our Lord and saviour,
He's reminding you he'll never fail yah,
He will deliver us
From this, and any other virus,
But we must have faith, pray, and trust.

Putin

There's no disputing that Vladimir Putin,
president of Russia
Has got Ukraine and other countries under
pressure;
His plan is to crush her,
And take their land - a treasure.
And is prepared to go to any measure
To expand and gain more land.
What a greedy man!

The excuses he uses,
Truly confuses.
His own people probably regret the hour
They voted him into power.
No matter how they plead,
He wants to see his enemies bleed.
His agenda
Is no retreat, no surrender.

No matter the sanctions,
Putin has shown no reaction.
No troops have been depleted,
Instead he's become more conceited.
He's remained defiant, and has not retreated.

So many crossing the border,
Creating chaos and disorder,
The last thing we need is another global catastrophe.
Some world leaders have simply gone crazy,
Will there ever be another peace treaty?
Only someone holy
Can end this calamity,
He owns every space,
No one's fit to tie his shoelace.
He will bring peace,
Then all evil and war will cease.

The Struggle Is Real GenZ

Generation Z rules the nation,
We're not toxic;
We'll weave our hair, or locks it,
Periodt always on our backs,
Our account they wanna hack.

Get off social media,
I hate what it feeds yah.

Relax mi dan,
I'm just on instagram,
Having a sic time with mi fam.

Why's your pants halfway down your waist,
Your speech is slurred and you walk at a slow pace.
In my time it would be short sharp shock,
And we started work at 7 o'clock.

Ancient like saying listen blood,
It's an old time story like Noah from the flood.
We're generation Z,
It's all about me, me, me.
Talking about that, let me just take a selfie;

Where’s the sympathy,
The stress we’re in, it’s the worst in history.
There’s pressure to choose an identity,
Bigender, transgender, or non-binary.
The need for clicks, and for likes to validate our status,
It's proof that people love or really hate us.
Education, isolation, pressure to wear the latest brand,
You’d have to be a millennial to really understand.
We were recently on meltdown,
Due to lockdown,
So many men down,
If you dwell on it, you’ll have a breakdown.

But we’re a bright and resilient bunch,
We made it through the credit crunch.
So many events and crisis,
Terrorist attacks, climate change, taliban now isis,
We’re generation z,
Making our mark in history.

D Mandem

When d mandem's on the road,
We're carrying a real heavy load,
Watching tings unfold;
Sometimes you gotta reload
To defend
The ends
Gold chain, chops bimma and Benz,
You gotta look out and watch your friends.

At night some roads are no go areas,
Our mums don't know where we are, but we're in their prayers.
We're no fools, we gotta look cool and act like players.
If the po po come, we just flee.
I hope and I pray they don't catch me,
I'm not like my friends, they fight like Mohammed Ali.
I can't float like a butterfly or sting like a bee,
In fact I'll head home to get some biscuit and tea.
This mandem lark is not for me,
I was brought up in a decent christian family;
I don't want to die like some mandem, I'm only 23.

Caught Up In The Madness

The madness, the madness
How can we escape this madness?
From the east to the west, badness and sadness,
Nation rising against nation,
Bringing stress and frustration.
Global warming, climate change,
Mentally, physically, some sexually deranged.
Economic nightmare pushing people to the edge,
Leaders and rulers retracting their pledge.
But we'll stick together and avoid the wedge
In this chaos and madness.

www.ingramcontent.com/pod-product-compliance
Lightning Source LLC
Chambersburg PA
CBHW051749130826
49812CB00033B/1060
* 9 7 8 9 3 5 7 2 1 3 1 9 6 *